THE **BIBLE** IN A **YEAR**
NOTEBOOK

Designed to be used with Ascension's *Bible in a Year* podcast with Fr. Mike Schmitz,

featuring Jeff Cavins

ASCENSION
West Chester, Pennsylvania

Ascension
PO Box 1990
West Chester, PA 19380

1-800-376-0520
ascensionpress.com

Cover design: Rosemary Strohm

Printed in the United States of America
21 22 23 24 25 5 4 3 2 1

ISBN 978-1-950784-72-1

The Bible in a Year Notebook

Walk through the entire Bible in 365 days!

What It Is

Based on the official 365-day reading plan from *The Bible in a Year* podcast with Fr. Mike Schmitz and Jeff Cavins, this notebook gives you space to write your reflections as you listen to Fr. Mike read the entire Bible, day by day.

With the notebook at your side as you listen to the podcast, you won't just read every word of the Bible in a year—you'll finally understand how all the pieces of the Bible fit together to tell an amazing story that continues in your life today.

How It Works

Every day, Fr. Mike reads two or three passages from Scripture. Then he leads listeners in prayer and offers some explanations and reflections. Jeff Cavins offers meaningful commentary that shows you the overarching narrative as you navigate through salvation history.

The Bible in a Year Notebook follows the plan Fr. Mike is using to read the entire Bible in 365 days. The notebook provides a place to write down your thoughts and prayers each day as you journey through the Bible.

Note the words that jump out at you as you listen to God's Word, take notes on Fr. Mike's reflections, and jot down your thoughts as you begin to see the world through the lens of Scripture.

The Great Adventure and *The Bible Timeline*

Unlike any other Bible podcast, Ascension's *Bible in a Year* follows a 365-day reading plan inspired by *The Great Adventure*® Bible Study Program's *Bible Timeline*® Learning System.

The Bible in a Year podcast is designed to help you find the story of what happened in the Bible—and discover how your life is part of the story.

Finding the Story

Have you tried to read the Bible before? Did you get lost in Leviticus?

Many people experience this problem because the Bible is unlike other books. In fact, the Bible is not really a "book" at all. It is a "library" of different kinds of literature, written over the span of about a thousand years by human authors under divine inspiration—to reveal God's plan of salvation.

Some of the books of the Bible are narrative books that tell the great story of humanity's creation, rebellion against God, and need for a savior. Other books in the Bible are books of poetry, wisdom, prophecy, law, and so forth. They are all God's Word, but not all tell the story. In fact, it is easy to lose the thread of the story if you simply read the books of the Bible in the order in which they appear.

How can you follow the story and understand the "big picture" that God communicates to us through the many people, places, and events? *The Bible Timeline* provides a way.

The Bible Timeline is a ground-breaking approach to understanding salvation history developed by renowned Catholic Bible scholar Jeff Cavins. *The Bible Timeline* divides the pages of the Bible into twelve time periods and shows how the different books fit into the time periods to tell the story.

Each *Great Adventure Bible Timeline* period has been assigned a color to represent what happened during this stage of the story of salvation:

Period	Color
Early World	Turquoise, the color of the earth viewed from space
Patriarchs	Burgundy, representing God's blood covenant with Abraham
Egypt and Exodus	Red, the color of the Red Sea
Desert Wanderings	Tan, the color of the desert
Conquest and Judges	Green, the color of the hills of Canaan
Royal Kingdom	Purple, the color of royalty
Divided Kingdom	Black, representing Israel's darkest period
Exile	Baby Blue, symbolizing Judah "singing the blues" in Babylon
Return	Yellow, symbolizing Judah's return home to brighter days
Maccabean Revolt	Orange, the color of the fire in the lamps in the purified Temple
Messianic Fulfillment	Gold, representing the gifts of the Magi
The Church	White, the color of the spotless Bride of Christ

Each day in *The Bible in a Year Notebook* is color-coded to match the time period of the Scripture readings for the day. As you journey through the 365-day reading plan, you will hear the story, told in the narrative books, and you will hear the books of wisdom and poetry and law, too. These books are arranged so you will encounter most of them at the same time you are reading the narrative book that tells the story of that time period.

Diving Deeper

On your journey through *The Bible in a Year*, you may appreciate Ascension's *Bible Timeline* Chart, a visual guide that shows how all the books of the Bible fit into these time periods. The chart shows where the people, places, and seventy key events of salvation history fit on the timeline in order to help you visualize the story. The chart also shows how God's family grew through a series of covenants, provides the genealogy of Jesus, and displays information about events in world history that occurred at the same time.

As you read the Word of God in Scripture, you may also begin to yearn for a deeper understanding of the story. *The Great Adventure* Bible Study Program, available from Ascension, uses *The Bible Timeline* to dive deeper into the drama of salvation history. More than a dozen studies are available to help you better understand the story of God's family and uncover the riches in the books of the Bible one by one. Visit ascensionpress.com for more information.

The Bible in a Year 365-Day Reading Plan

		Period	First Reading	Second Reading	Psalms/Proverbs/ Song
		NOTE: Readings in bold are from the 14 narrative books of the Bible. *Psalms in italics* are connected to the first readings.			
☐	Day 1	Early World	**Genesis 1–2**		*Psalm 19*
☐	Day 2		**Genesis 3–4**		*Psalm 104*
☐	Day 3		**Genesis 5–6**		*Psalm 136*
☐	Day 4		**Genesis 7–9**		Psalm 1
☐	Day 5		**Genesis 10–11**		Psalm 2
☐	Day 6	Patriarchs	**Genesis 12–13**	Job 1–2	Proverbs 1:1-7
☐	Day 7		**Genesis 14–15**	Job 3–4	Proverbs 1:8-19
☐	Day 8		**Genesis 16–17**	Job 5–6	Proverbs 1:20-33
☐	Day 9		**Genesis 18–19**	Job 7–8	Proverbs 2:1-5
☐	Day 10		**Genesis 20–21**	Job 9–10	Proverbs 2:6-8
☐	Day 11		**Genesis 22–23**	Job 11–12	Proverbs 2:9-15
☐	Day 12		**Genesis 24**	Job 13–14	Proverbs 2:16-19
☐	Day 13		**Genesis 25–26**	Job 15–16	Proverbs 2:20-22
☐	Day 14		**Genesis 27–28**	Job 17–18	Proverbs 3:1-4
☐	Day 15		**Genesis 29–30**	Job 19–20	Proverbs 3:5-8
☐	Day 16		**Genesis 31–32**	Job 21–22	Proverbs 3:9-12
☐	Day 17		**Genesis 33–34**	Job 23–24	Proverbs 3:13-18

		Period	First Reading	Second Reading	Psalms/Proverbs/Song
❏	Day 18		**Genesis 35–36**	Job 25–26	Proverbs 3:19-24
❏	Day 19		**Genesis 37**	Job 27–28	Proverbs 3:25-27
❏	Day 20		**Genesis 38**	Job 29–30	Proverbs 3:28-32
❏	Day 21		**Genesis 39–40**	Job 31–32	Proverbs 3:33-35
❏	Day 22	Patriarchs	**Genesis 41–42**	Job 33–34	Proverbs 4:1-9
❏	Day 23		**Genesis 43–44**	Job 35–36	Proverbs 4:10 19
❏	Day 24		**Genesis 45–46**	Job 37–38	Proverbs 4:20-27
❏	Day 25		**Genesis 47–48**	Job 39–40	Psalm 16
❏	Day 26		**Genesis 49–50**	Job 41–42	Psalm 17
❏	Day 27		**Exodus 1–2**	Leviticus 1	Psalm 44
❏	Day 28		**Exodus 3**	Leviticus 2–3	Psalm 45
❏	Day 29		**Exodus 4–5**	Leviticus 4	Psalm 46
❏	Day 30		**Exodus 6–7**	Leviticus 5	Psalm 47
❏	Day 31		**Exodus 8**	Leviticus 6	Psalm 48
❏	Day 32		**Exodus 9**	Leviticus 7	Psalm 49
❏	Day 33	Egypt and Exodus	**Exodus 10–11**	Leviticus 8	Psalm 50
❏	Day 34		**Exodus 12**	Leviticus 9	*Psalm 114*
❏	Day 35		**Exodus 13–14**	Leviticus 10	Psalm 53
❏	Day 36		**Exodus 15–16**	Leviticus 11	Psalm 71
❏	Day 37		**Exodus 17–18**	Leviticus 12	Psalm 73
❏	Day 38		**Exodus 19–20**	Leviticus 13	Psalm 74
❏	Day 39		**Exodus 21**	Leviticus 14	Psalm 75

		Period	First Reading	Second Reading	Psalms/Proverbs/Song
❏	Day 40	Egypt and Exodus	Exodus 22	Leviticus 15	Psalm 76
❏	Day 41		Exodus 23	Leviticus 16	Psalm 77
❏	Day 42		Exodus 24	Leviticus 17–18	Psalm 78
❏	Day 43		Exodus 25–26	Leviticus 19	*Psalm 119:1-56*
❏	Day 44		Exodus 27–28	Leviticus 20	*Psalm 119:57-120*
❏	Day 45		Exodus 29	Leviticus 21	*Psalm 119:121-176*
❏	Day 46		Exodus 30–31	Leviticus 22	*Psalm 115*
❏	Day 47		Exodus 32	Leviticus 23	Psalm 79
❏	Day 48		Exodus 33–34	Leviticus 24	Psalm 80
❏	Day 49		Exodus 35–36	Leviticus 25	Psalm 81
❏	Day 50		Exodus 37–38	Leviticus 26	Psalm 82
❏	Day 51		Exodus 39–40	Leviticus 27	Psalm 83
❏	Day 52	Desert Wanderings	Numbers 1	Deuteronomy 1	Psalm 84
❏	Day 53		Numbers 2	Deuteronomy 2	Psalm 85
❏	Day 54		Numbers 3	Deuteronomy 3	Psalm 87
❏	Day 55		Numbers 4	Deuteronomy 4	Psalm 88
❏	Day 56		Numbers 5	Deuteronomy 5	Psalm 90
❏	Day 57		Numbers 6	Deuteronomy 6	Psalm 91
❏	Day 58		Numbers 7	Deuteronomy 7	Psalm 92
❏	Day 59		Numbers 8–9	Deuteronomy 8	Psalm 93
❏	Day 60		Numbers 10	Deuteronomy 9	Psalm 10
❏	Day 61		Numbers 11	Deuteronomy 10	Psalm 33

		Period	First Reading	Second Reading	Psalms/Proverbs/Song
❏	Day 62		**Numbers 12–13**	Deuteronomy 11	Psalm 94
❏	Day 63		**Numbers 14**	Deuteronomy 12	Psalm 95
❏	Day 64		**Numbers 15**	Deuteronomy 13–14	Psalm 96
❏	Day 65		**Numbers 16**	Deuteronomy 15–16	Psalm 97
❏	Day 66		**Numbers 17**	Deuteronomy 17–18	Psalm 98
❏	Day 67		**Numbers 18**	Deuteronomy 19–20	Psalm 99
❏	Day 68		**Numbers 19–20**	Deuteronomy 21	Psalm 100
❏	Day 69		**Numbers 21**	Deuteronomy 22	Psalm 102
❏	Day 70		**Numbers 22**	Deuteronomy 23	Psalm 105
❏	Day 71	**Desert Wanderings**	**Numbers 23**	Deuteronomy 24–25	Psalm 106
❏	Day 72		**Numbers 24–25**	Deuteronomy 26	Psalm 107
❏	Day 73		**Numbers 26**	Deuteronomy 27	Psalm 111
❏	Day 74		**Numbers 27–28**	Deuteronomy 28	Psalm 112
❏	Day 75		**Numbers 29–30**	Deuteronomy 29	Psalm 113
❏	Day 76		**Numbers 31**	Deuteronomy 30	Psalm 116
❏	Day 77		**Numbers 32**	Deuteronomy 31	Psalm 117
❏	Day 78		**Numbers 33**	Deuteronomy 32	Psalm 118
❏	Day 79		**Numbers 34**	Deuteronomy 33	Psalm 120
❏	Day 80		**Numbers 35–36**	Deuteronomy 34	Psalm 121
❏	Day 81		**Joshua 1–4**		Psalm 123
❏	Day 82	**Conquest and Judges**	**Joshua 5–7**		Psalm 125
❏	Day 83		**Joshua 8–9**		Psalm 126

		Period	First Reading	Second Reading	Psalms/Proverbs/Song
❐	Day 84		**Joshua 10–11**		Psalm 128
❐	Day 85		**Joshua 12–14**		Psalm 129
❐	Day 86		**Joshua 15–18**		Psalm 130
❐	Day 87		**Joshua 19–21**		Psalm 131
❐	Day 88		**Joshua 22–24**		Psalm 132
❐	Day 89		**Judges 1–3**	Ruth 1	Psalm 133
❐	Day 90		**Judges 4–5**	Ruth 2	Psalm 134
❐	Day 91	Conquest and Judges	**Judges 6–8**	Ruth 3	Psalm 135
❐	Day 92		**Judges 9–11**	Ruth 4	Psalm 137
❐	Day 93		**Judges 12–15**		Psalm 146
❐	Day 94		**Judges 16–18**		Psalm 147
❐	Day 95		**Judges 19–21**		Psalm 148
❐	Day 96		**1 Samuel 1–2**		Psalm 149
❐	Day 97		**1 Samuel 3–5**		Psalm 150
❐	Day 98		**1 Samuel 6–8**		*Psalm 86*
❐	Day 99		John 1–3		Proverbs 5:1-6
❐	Day 100		John 4–6		Proverbs 5:7-14
❐	Day 101		John 7–9		Proverbs 5:15-23
❐	Day 102	Messianic Checkpoint	John 10–12		Proverbs 6:1-5
❐	Day 103		John 13–15		Proverbs 6:6-11
❐	Day 104		John 16–18		Proverbs 6:12-15
❐	Day 105		John 19–21		Proverbs 6:16-22

		Period	First Reading	Second Reading	Psalms/Proverbs/Song
❒	Day 106		**1 Samuel 9–10**		Proverbs 6:23-35
❒	Day 107		**1 Samuel 11–12**		Psalm 55
❒	Day 108		**1 Samuel 13–14**		Psalm 58
❒	Day 109		**1 Samuel 15–16**		Psalm 61
❒	Day 110		**1 Samuel 17**		Psalm 12
❒	Day 111		**1 Samuel 18–19**		*Psalm 59*
❒	Day 112		**1 Samuel 20**		*Psalm 142*
❒	Day 113		**1 Samuel 21–22**		*Psalm 52*
❒	Day 114		**1 Samuel 23**		*Psalm 54*
❒	Day 115		**1 Samuel 24**		*Psalm 57*
❒	Day 116	Royal Kingdom	**1 Samuel 25**		*Psalm 63*
❒	Day 117		**1 Samuel 26**		*Psalm 56*
❒	Day 118		**1 Samuel 27–28**		*Psalm 34*
❒	Day 119		**1 Samuel 29–31**		*Psalm 18*
❒	Day 120		**2 Samuel 1**	1 Chronicles 1	Psalm 13
❒	Day 121		**2 Samuel 2**	1 Chronicles 2	Psalm 24
❒	Day 122		**2 Samuel 3**	1 Chronicles 3–4	Psalm 25
❒	Day 123		**2 Samuel 4**	1 Chronicles 5–6	Psalm 26
❒	Day 124		**2 Samuel 5**	1 Chronicles 7–8	Psalm 27
❒	Day 125		**2 Samuel 6–7**	1 Chronicles 9	*Psalm 89*
❒	Day 126		**2 Samuel 8**	1 Chronicles 10–11	*Psalm 60*
❒	Day 127		**2 Samuel 9**	1 Chronicles 12	Psalm 28

		Period	First Reading	Second Reading	Psalms/Proverbs/ Song
❏	Day 128		**2 Samuel 10**	1 Chronicles 13	Psalm 31
❏	Day 129		**2 Samuel 11**	1 Chronicles 14–15	Psalm 32
❏	Day 130		**2 Samuel 12**	1 Chronicles 16	*Psalm 51*
❏	Day 131		**2 Samuel 13**	1 Chronicles 17	Psalm 35
❏	Day 132		**2 Samuel 14**	1 Chronicles 18	Psalm 14
❏	Day 133		**2 Samuel 15**	1 Chronicles 19–20	*Psalm 3*
❏	Day 134		**2 Samuel 16**	1 Chronicles 21	Psalm 15
❏	Day 135		**2 Samuel 17**	1 Chronicles 22	Psalm 36
❏	Day 136		**2 Samuel 18**	1 Chronicles 23	Psalm 37
❏	Day 137		**2 Samuel 19**	1 Chronicles 24	Psalm 38
❏	Day 138		**2 Samuel 20**	1 Chronicles 25	Psalm 39
❏	Day 139	Royal Kingdom	**2 Samuel 21**	1 Chronicles 26	Psalm 40
❏	Day 140		**2 Samuel 22**	1 Chronicles 27	Psalm 41
❏	Day 141		**2 Samuel 23**	1 Chronicles 28	Psalm 42
❏	Day 142		**2 Samuel 24**	1 Chronicles 29	*Psalm 30*
❏	Day 143		**1 Kings 1**	2 Chronicles 1	Psalm 43
❏	Day 144		**1 Kings 2**	2 Chronicles 2–3	Psalm 62
❏	Day 145		**1 Kings 3**	2 Chronicles 4–5	Psalm 64
❏	Day 146		**1 Kings 4**	2 Chronicles 6	Psalm 65
❏	Day 147		**1 Kings 5**	2 Chronicles 7–8	Psalm 66
❏	Day 148		**1 Kings 6**	2 Chronicles 9	Psalm 4
❏	Day 149		**1 Kings 7**	Ecclesiastes 1–2	Psalm 5

		Period	First Reading	Second Reading	Psalms/Proverbs/Song
❐	Day 150	**Royal Kingdom**	**1 Kings 8**	Ecclesiastes 3–5	Psalm 6
❐	Day 151		**1 Kings 9**	Ecclesiastes 6–7	Psalm 7
❐	Day 152		**1 Kings 10**	Ecclesiastes 8–9	Psalm 8
❐	Day 153		**1 Kings 11**	Ecclesiastes 10–12	Psalm 9
❐	Day 154	**Messianic Checkpoint**	Mark 1–2		Psalm 11
❐	Day 155		Mark 3–4		Psalm 20
❐	Day 156		Mark 5–6		Psalm 21
❐	Day 157		Mark 7–8		Psalm 23
❐	Day 158		Mark 9–10		Psalm 29
❐	Day 159		Mark 11–12		Psalm 67
❐	Day 160		Mark 13–14		Psalm 68
❐	Day 161		Mark 15–16		*Psalm 22*
❐	Day 162	**Divided Kingdom**	**1 Kings 12**	2 Chronicles 10–11	Song of Solomon 1
❐	Day 163		**1 Kings 13**	2 Chronicles 12–13	Song of Solomon 2
❐	Day 164		**1 Kings 14**	2 Chronicles 14–15	Song of Solomon 3
❐	Day 165		**1 Kings 15–16**	2 Chronicles 16–17	Song of Solomon 4
❐	Day 166		**1 Kings 17–18**	2 Chronicles 18–19	Song of Solomon 5
❐	Day 167		**1 Kings 19–20**	2 Chronicles 20	Song of Solomon 6
❐	Day 168		**1 Kings 21**	2 Chronicles 21–22	Song of Solomon 7
❐	Day 169		**1 Kings 22**	2 Chronicles 23	Song of Solomon 8
❐	Day 170		**2 Kings 1**	2 Chronicles 24	Psalm 69
❐	Day 171		**2 Kings 2**	2 Chronicles 25	Psalm 70

		Period	First Reading	Second Reading	Psalms/Proverbs/Song
❏	Day 172		**2 Kings 3**	2 Chronicles 26–27	Psalm 72
❏	Day 173		**2 Kings 4**	2 Chronicles 28	Psalm 127
❏	Day 174		**2 Kings 5**	Hosea 1–3	Psalm 101
❏	Day 175		**2 Kings 6–7**	Hosea 4–7	Psalm 103
❏	Day 176		**2 Kings 8**	Hosea 8–10	Psalm 108
❏	Day 177		**2 Kings 9**	Hosea 11–14	Psalm 109
❏	Day 178	Divided Kingdom	**2 Kings 10**	Amos 1–3	Psalm 110
❏	Day 179		**2 Kings 11–12**	Amos 4–6	Psalm 122
❏	Day 180		**2 Kings 13–14**	Amos 7–9	Psalm 124
❏	Day 181		**2 Kings 15**	Jonah 1–4	Psalm 138
❏	Day 182		**2 Kings 16**	Micah 1–4	Psalm 139
❏	Day 183		**2 Kings 17**	Micah 5–7	Psalm 140
❏	Day 184		**2 Kings 18**	2 Chronicles 29	Psalm 141
❏	Day 185		**2 Kings 19**	2 Chronicles 30	Psalm 143
❏	Day 186		**2 Kings 20**	2 Chronicles 31	Psalm 144
❏	Day 187		**2 Kings 21**	2 Chronicles 32	Psalm 145
❏	Day 188	Exile	**2 Kings 22**	2 Chronicles 33	Proverbs 7
❏	Day 189		**2 Kings 23**	2 Chronicles 34	Proverbs 8:1-21
❏	Day 190		**2 Kings 24**	2 Chronicles 35	Proverbs 8:22-36
❏	Day 191		**2 Kings 25**	2 Chronicles 36	Proverbs 9:1-6
❏	Day 192		Isaiah 1–2	Tobit 1–2	Proverbs 9:7-12
❏	Day 193		Isaiah 3–4	Tobit 3–4	Proverbs 9:13-18

		Period	First Reading	Second Reading	Psalms/Proverbs/Song
❑	Day 194		Isaiah 5–6	Tobit 5–6	Proverbs 10:1-4
❑	Day 195		Isaiah 7–8	Tobit 7–9	Proverbs 10:5-8
❑	Day 196		Isaiah 9–10	Tobit 10–12	Proverbs 10:9-12
❑	Day 197		Isaiah 11–13	Tobit 13–14	Proverbs 10:13-16
❑	Day 198		Isaiah 14–15	Joel 1–2	Proverbs 10:17-20
❑	Day 199		Isaiah 16–17	Joel 3	Proverbs 10:21-24
❑	Day 200		Isaiah 18–20	Nahum 1–2	Proverbs 10:25-28
❑	Day 201		Isaiah 21–22	Nahum 3	Proverbs 10:29-32
❑	Day 202		Isaiah 23–24	Habakkuk 1–2	Proverbs 11:1-4
❑	Day 203		Isaiah 25–27	Habakkuk 3	Proverbs 11:5-8
❑	Day 204	Exile	Isaiah 28–29	Zephaniah 1–2	Proverbs 11:9-12
❑	Day 205		Isaiah 30–31	Zephaniah 3	Proverbs 11:13-16
❑	Day 206		Isaiah 32–33	Baruch 1–2	Proverbs 11:17-20
❑	Day 207		Isaiah 34–36	Baruch 3–4	Proverbs 11:21-24
❑	Day 208		Isaiah 37–38	Baruch 5–6	Proverbs 11:25-28
❑	Day 209		Isaiah 39–40	Ezekiel 1	Proverbs 11:29-31
❑	Day 210		Isaiah 41–42	Ezekiel 2–3	Proverbs 12:1-4
❑	Day 211		Isaiah 43–44	Ezekiel 4–5	Proverbs 12:5-8
❑	Day 212		Isaiah 45–46	Ezekiel 6–7	Proverbs 12:9-12
❑	Day 213		Isaiah 47–48	Ezekiel 8–9	Proverbs 12:13-16
❑	Day 214		Isaiah 49–50	Ezekiel 10–11	Proverbs 12:17-20
❑	Day 215		Isaiah 51–52	Ezekiel 12–13	Proverbs 12:21-24
❑	Day 216		Isaiah 53–54	Ezekiel 14–15	Proverbs 12:25-28

		Period	First Reading	Second Reading	Psalms/Proverbs/ Song
❐	Day 217		Isaiah 55–56	Ezekiel 16	Proverbs 13:1-4
❐	Day 218		Isaiah 57–58	Ezekiel 17–18	Proverbs 13:5-8
❐	Day 219		Isaiah 59–60	Ezekiel 19	Proverbs 13:9-12
❐	Day 220		Isaiah 61–62	Ezekiel 20	Proverbs 13:13-16
❐	Day 221		Isaiah 63–64	Ezekiel 21–22	Proverbs 13:17-20
❐	Day 222		Isaiah 65	Ezekiel 23–24	Proverbs 13:21-25
❐	Day 223		Isaiah 66	Ezekiel 25–26	Proverbs 14:1-4
❐	Day 224		Jeremiah 1	Ezekiel 27	Proverbs 14:5-8
❐	Day 225		Jeremiah 2	Ezekiel 28	Proverbs 14:9-12
❐	Day 226		Jeremiah 3	Ezekiel 29–30	Proverbs 14:13-16
❐	Day 227	Exile	Jeremiah 4	Ezekiel 31–32	Proverbs 14:17-20
❐	Day 228		Jeremiah 5	Ezekiel 33	Proverbs 14:21-24
❐	Day 229		Jeremiah 6	Ezekiel 34–35	Proverbs 14:25-28
❐	Day 230		Jeremiah 7	Ezekiel 36	Proverbs 14:29-32
❐	Day 231		Jeremiah 8	Ezekiel 37–38	Proverbs 14:33-35
❐	Day 232		Jeremiah 9	Ezekiel 39	Proverbs 15:1-4
❐	Day 233		Jeremiah 10–11	Ezekiel 40	Proverbs 15:5-8
❐	Day 234		Jeremiah 12–13	Ezekiel 41–42	Proverbs 15:9-12
❐	Day 235		Jeremiah 14–15	Ezekiel 43–44	Proverbs 15:13-16
❐	Day 236		Jeremiah 16–17	Ezekiel 45–46	Proverbs 15:17-20
❐	Day 237		Jeremiah 18–19	Ezekiel 47–48	Proverbs 15:21-24
❐	Day 238		Jeremiah 20–21	Daniel 1–2	Proverbs 15:25-28
❐	Day 239		Jeremiah 22	Daniel 3	Proverbs 15:29-33

	Period	First Reading	Second Reading	Psalms/Proverbs/Song
❐ Day 240		Jeremiah 23	Daniel 4–5	Proverbs 16:1-4
❐ Day 241		Jeremiah 24–25	Daniel 6–7	Proverbs 16:5-8
❐ Day 242		Jeremiah 26–27	Daniel 8–9	Proverbs 16:9-12
❐ Day 243		Jeremiah 28–29	Daniel 10–11	Proverbs 16:13-16
❐ Day 244		Jeremiah 30	Daniel 12–13	Proverbs 16:17-20
❐ Day 245		Jeremiah 31	Daniel 14	Proverbs 16:21-24
❐ Day 246		Jeremiah 32	Judith 1–2	Proverbs 16:25-28
❐ Day 247		Jeremiah 33–34	Judith 3–5	Proverbs 16:29-33
❐ Day 248	Exile	Jeremiah 35–36	Judith 6–7	Proverbs 17:1-4
❐ Day 249		Jeremiah 37–38	Judith 8–9	Proverbs 17:5-8
❐ Day 250		Jeremiah 39–40	Judith 10–11	Proverbs 17:9-12
❐ Day 251		Jeremiah 41–42	Judith 12–14	Proverbs 17:13-16
❐ Day 252		Jeremiah 43–44	Judith 15–16	Proverbs 17:17-20
❐ Day 253		Jeremiah 45–46	Lamentations 1	Proverbs 17:21-28
❐ Day 254		Jeremiah 47–48	Lamentations 2	Proverbs 18:1-4
❐ Day 255		Jeremiah 49–50	Lamentations 3	Proverbs 18:5-8
❐ Day 256		Jeremiah 51	Lamentations 4–5	Proverbs 18:9-12
❐ Day 257		Jeremiah 52	Obadiah	Proverbs 18:13-16
❐ Day 258		Matthew 1–4		Proverbs 18:17-20
❐ Day 259	Messianic Checkpoint	Matthew 5–7		Proverbs 18:21-24
❐ Day 260		Matthew 8–10		Proverbs 19:1-4
❐ Day 261		Matthew 11–13		Proverbs 19:5-8

		Period	First Reading	Second Reading	Psalms/Proverbs/Song
❐	Day 262		Matthew 14–17		Proverbs 19:9-12
❐	Day 263		Matthew 18–21		Proverbs 19:13-16
❐	Day 264	Messianic Checkpoint	Matthew 22–24		Proverbs 19:17-20
❐	Day 265		Matthew 25–26		Proverbs 19:21-24
❐	Day 266		Matthew 27–28		Proverbs 19:25-29
❐	Day 267		**Ezra 1–2**	Haggai 1–2	Proverbs 20:1-3
❐	Day 268		**Ezra 3–4**	Zechariah 1–3	Proverbs 20:4-7
❐	Day 269		**Ezra 5–6**	Zechariah 4–6	Proverbs 20:8-11
❐	Day 270		**Ezra 7–8**	Zechariah 7–8	Proverbs 20:12-15
❐	Day 271		**Ezra 9–10**	Zechariah 9–11	Proverbs 20:16-19
❐	Day 272		**Nehemiah 1–2**	Zechariah 12–13	Proverbs 20:20-22
❐	Day 273		**Nehemiah 3**	Zechariah 14	Proverbs 20:23-26
❐	Day 274	Return	**Nehemiah 4–5**	Esther 11–12	Proverbs 20:27-30
❐	Day 275		**Nehemiah 6–7**	Esther 1–2	Proverbs 21:1-4
❐	Day 276		**Nehemiah 8**	Esther 3, 13	Proverbs 21:5-8
❐	Day 277		**Nehemiah 9**	Esther 4, 14	Proverbs 21:9-12
❐	Day 278		**Nehemiah 10**	Esther 15, 6–7	Proverbs 21:13-16
❐	Day 279		**Nehemiah 11**	Esther 8, 16	Proverbs 21:17-20
❐	Day 280		**Nehemiah 12**	Esther 9–11	Proverbs 21:21-24
❐	Day 281		**Nehemiah 13**	Malachi 1–4	Proverbs 21:25-28
❐	Day 282	Maccabean Revolt	**1 Maccabees 1**	Sirach 1–3	Proverbs 21:29-31
❐	Day 283		**1 Maccabees 2**	Sirach 4–6	Proverbs 22:1-4

		Period	First Reading	Second Reading	Psalms/Proverbs/Song
❏	Day 284		**1 Maccabees 3**	Sirach 7–9	Proverbs 22:5-8
❏	Day 285		**1 Maccabees 4**	Sirach 10–12	Proverbs 22:9-12
❏	Day 286		**1 Maccabees 5**	Sirach 13–15	Proverbs 22:13-16
❏	Day 287		**1 Maccabees 6**	Sirach 16–18	Proverbs 22:17-21
❏	Day 288		**1 Maccabees 7**	Sirach 19–21	Proverbs 22:22-25
❏	Day 289		**1 Maccabees 8**	Sirach 22 23	Proverbs 22:26-29
❏	Day 290		**1 Maccabees 9**	Sirach 24–25	Proverbs 23:1-4
❏	Day 291		**1 Maccabees 10**	Sirach 26–27	Proverbs 23:5-8
❏	Day 292		**1 Maccabees 11**	Sirach 28–29	Proverbs 23:9-12
❏	Day 293		**1 Maccabees 12**	Sirach 30–31	Proverbs 23:13-16
❏	Day 294		**1 Maccabees 13**	Sirach 32–33	Proverbs 23:17-21
❏	Day 295	**Maccabean Revolt**	**1 Maccabees 14**	Sirach 34–35	Proverbs 23:22-25
❏	Day 296		**1 Maccabees 15**	Sirach 36–37	Proverbs 23:26-28
❏	Day 297		**1 Maccabees 16**	Sirach 38–39	Proverbs 23:29-35
❏	Day 298		2 Maccabees 1	Sirach 40–41	Proverbs 24:1-7
❏	Day 299		2 Maccabees 2	Sirach 42–44	Proverbs 24:8-9
❏	Day 300		2 Maccabees 3	Sirach 45–46	Proverbs 24:10-12
❏	Day 301		2 Maccabees 4	Sirach 47–49	Proverbs 24:13-16
❏	Day 302		2 Maccabees 5	Sirach 50–51	Proverbs 24:17-20
❏	Day 303		2 Maccabees 6	Wisdom 1–2	Proverbs 24:21-26
❏	Day 304		2 Maccabees 7	Wisdom 3–4	Proverbs 24:27-29
❏	Day 305		2 Maccabees 8	Wisdom 5–6	Proverbs 24:30-34

		Period	First Reading	Second Reading	Psalms/Proverbs/Song
❏	Day 306	Maccabean Revolt	2 Maccabees 9	Wisdom 7–8	Proverbs 25:1-3
❏	Day 307		2 Maccabees 10	Wisdom 9–10	Proverbs 25:4-7
❏	Day 308		2 Maccabees 11	Wisdom 11–12	Proverbs 25:8-10
❏	Day 309		2 Maccabees 12	Wisdom 13–14	Proverbs 25:11-14
❏	Day 310		2 Maccabees 13	Wisdom 15–16	Proverbs 25:15-17
❏	Day 311		2 Maccabees 14	Wisdom 17–18	Proverbs 25:18-20
❏	Day 312		2 Maccabees 15	Wisdom 19	Proverbs 25:21-23
❏	Day 313	Messianic Fulfillment	Luke 1–2		Proverbs 25:24-26
❏	Day 314		Luke 3–5		Proverbs 25:27-28
❏	Day 315		Luke 6–8		Proverbs 26:1-3
❏	Day 316		Luke 9–10		Proverbs 26:4-6
❏	Day 317		Luke 11–12		Proverbs 26:7-9
❏	Day 318		Luke 13–16		Proverbs 26:10-12
❏	Day 319		Luke 17–19		Proverbs 26:13-16
❏	Day 320		Luke 20–22:38		Proverbs 26:17-19
❏	Day 321		Luke 22:39–24:50		Proverbs 26:20-23
❏	Day 322	The Church	Acts 1	Romans 1	Proverbs 26:24-26
❏	Day 323		Acts 2	Romans 2–3	Proverbs 26:27-28
❏	Day 324		Acts 3	Romans 4–5	Proverbs 27:1-3
❏	Day 325		Acts 4	Romans 6–7	Proverbs 27:4-6
❏	Day 326		Acts 5	Romans 8	Proverbs 27:7-9
❏	Day 327		Acts 6	Romans 9–10	Proverbs 27:10-12

		Period	First Reading	Second Reading	Psalms/Proverbs/Song
☐	Day 328		Acts 7	Romans 11–12	Proverbs 27:13-14
☐	Day 329		Acts 8	Romans 13–14	Proverbs 27:15-17
☐	Day 330		Acts 9	Romans 15–16	Proverbs 27:18-20
☐	Day 331		Acts 10	1 Corinthians 1–2	Proverbs 27:21-22
☐	Day 332		Acts 11	1 Corinthians 3–4	Proverbs 27:23-27
☐	Day 333		Acts 12	1 Corinthians 5–6	Proverbs 28:1 3
☐	Day 334		Acts 13	1 Corinthians 7–8	Proverbs 28:4-6
☐	Day 335		Acts 14	1 Corinthians 9–10	Proverbs 28:7-9
☐	Day 336		Acts 15	1 Corinthians 11–12	Proverbs 28:10-12
☐	Day 337		Acts 16	1 Corinthians 13–14	Proverbs 28:13-15
☐	Day 338		Acts 17	1 Corinthians 15	Proverbs 28:16-18
☐	Day 339	The Church	Acts 18	1 Corinthians 16	Proverbs 28:19-21
☐	Day 340		Acts 19	2 Corinthians 1–2	Proverbs 28:22-24
☐	Day 341		Acts 20	2 Corinthians 3–5	Proverbs 28:25-28
☐	Day 342		Acts 21	2 Corinthians 6–8	Proverbs 29:1-4
☐	Day 343		Acts 22	2 Corinthians 9–11	Proverbs 29:5-7
☐	Day 344		Acts 23	2 Corinthians 12–13	Proverbs 29:8-11
☐	Day 345		Acts 24	Galatians 1–3	Proverbs 29:12-14
☐	Day 346		Acts 25	Galatians 4–6	Proverbs 29:15-17
☐	Day 347		Acts 26	Ephesians 1–3	Proverbs 29:18-21
☐	Day 348		Acts 27	Ephesians 4–6	Proverbs 29:22-24
☐	Day 349		Acts 28	Philippians 1–2	Proverbs 29:25-27

	Period	First Reading	Second Reading	Psalms/Proverbs/Song
❒ Day 350	The Church	James 1–2	Philippians 3–4	Proverbs 30:1-6
❒ Day 351		James 3–5	Colossians 1–2	Proverbs 30:7-9
❒ Day 352		1 Peter 1–2	Colossians 3–4	Proverbs 30:10-14
❒ Day 353		1 Peter 3–5	1 Thessalonians 1–3	Proverbs 30:15-16
❒ Day 354		2 Peter 1–3	1 Thessalonians 4–5	Proverbs 30:17-19
❒ Day 355		1 John 1–3	2 Thessalonians 1–3	Proverbs 30:20-23
❒ Day 356		1 John 4–5	1 Timothy 1–3	Proverbs 30:24-28
❒ Day 357		2 John, 3 John	1 Timothy 4–6	Proverbs 30:29-33
❒ Day 358		Jude	2 Timothy 1–2	Proverbs 31:1-7
❒ Day 359		Revelation 1–3	2 Timothy 3–4	Proverbs 31:8-9
❒ Day 360		Revelation 4–7	Titus 1–3	Proverbs 31:10-15
❒ Day 361		Revelation 8–11	Philemon	Proverbs 31:16-18
❒ Day 362		Revelation 12–14	Hebrews 1–4	Proverbs 31:19-22
❒ Day 363		Revelation 15–17	Hebrews 5–8	Proverbs 31:23-25
❒ Day 364		Revelation 18–20	Hebrews 9–10	Proverbs 31:26-29
❒ Day 365		Revelation 21–22	Hebrews 11–13	Proverbs 31:30-31

Early World

Creation to 2200 BC

The Bible begins when God creates the world. Man is created in God's image, but Adam and Eve, the first man and woman, disobey God, and sin enters the world. God does not abandon his people but promises a savior. After the Flood, he makes a covenant with Noah, expanding the family of God.

_____

_____

_____

_____

_____

_____

_____

_____

_____

_____

_____

_____

created out of "nothing" — out of God's sheer
goodness —
Catechism →
creation not to be taken literally

What do you see through the lens of Scripture?

Give first fruits

where did Cain find a wife

Genesis 5–6   *Psalm 136*

How can I walk w/ God

What do you see through the lens of Scripture?

Genesis 7–9   *Psalm 1*

What do you see through the lens of Scripture?

Patriarchs

2200 BC to 1800 BC

Abraham, Isaac, Jacob, and Jacob's twelve sons are the fathers, or patriarchs, of ancient Israel. The story of this period begins with the call of Abraham and continues as the family of Jacob, who is also called Israel, settles in Egypt.

Genesis 12–13   Job 1–2   Proverbs 1:1-7

_____

_____

_____

_____

_____

_____

_____

What do you see through the lens of Scripture?

Genesis 14–15   Job 3–4   Proverbs 1:8-19

_____

_____

_____

_____

_____

_____

_____

DAY 8

Genesis 16–17   Job 5–6   Proverbs 1:20-33

What do you see through the lens of Scripture?

DAY 9

Genesis 18–19   Job 7–8   Proverbs 2:1-5

Genesis 20–21   Job 9–10   Proverbs 2:6-8

_____

_____

_____

_____

_____

_____

What do you see through the lens of Scripture?

Genesis 22–23   Job 11–12   Proverbs 2:9-15

_____

_____

_____

_____

_____

_____

Genesis 24   Job 13–14   Proverbs 2:16-19

_____
_____
_____
_____
_____
_____
_____

What do you see through the lens of Scripture?

Genesis 25–26   Job 15–16   Proverbs 2:20-22

_____
_____
_____
_____
_____
_____
_____

Genesis 27–28   Job 17–18   Proverbs 3:1-4

_____

_____

_____

_____

_____

_____

_____

What do you see through the lens of Scripture?

Genesis 29–30   Job 19–20   Proverbs 3:5-8

_____

_____

_____

_____

_____

_____

_____

DAY 16

Genesis 31–32　　　　　Job 21–22　　　　　Proverbs 3:9-12

_____
_____
_____
_____
_____
_____
_____

What do you see through the lens of Scripture?

DAY 17

Genesis 33–34　　　　　Job 23–24　　　　　Proverbs 3:13-18

_____
_____
_____
_____
_____
_____
_____

Genesis 35–36   Job 25–26   Proverbs 3:19-24

Benjamin born

What do you see through the lens of Scripture?

Genesis 37   Job 27–28   Proverbs 3:25-27

DAY 18

DAY 19

Genesis 38   Job 29–30   Proverbs 3:28-32

_____
_____
_____
_____
_____
_____
_____

What do you see through the lens of Scripture?

Genesis 39–40   Job 31–32   Proverbs 3:33-35

_____
_____
_____
_____
_____
_____

Genesis 41–42   Job 33–34   Proverbs 4:1-9

DAY 22

_____
_____
_____
_____
_____
_____
_____

What do you see through the lens of Scripture?

Genesis 43–44   Job 35–36   Proverbs 4:10-19

DAY 23

_____
_____
_____
_____
_____
_____
_____

Genesis 45–46   Job 37–38   Proverbs 4:20-27

_____

_____

_____

_____

_____

_____

_____

What do you see through the lens of Scripture?

Genesis 47–48   Job 39–40   Psalm 16

_____

_____

_____

_____

_____

_____

_____

What do you see through the lens of Scripture?

Egypt and Exodus

1800 BC to 1446 BC

The story of the third biblical time period begins with Jacob (Israel) and his family living in the land of Egypt, where a new pharaoh has made them slaves. After a series of plagues, Pharaoh frees the Israelites, and Moses parts the Red Sea. God reveals the Ten Commandments and makes a covenant at Mount Sinai with Moses.

_____

_____

_____

_____

_____

_____

_____

_____

_____

_____

_____

_____

Exodus 1–2   Leviticus 1   Psalm 44

D
A
Y

2
7

_____

_____

_____

_____

_____

_____

_____

What do you see through the lens of Scripture?

Exodus 3   Leviticus 2–3   Psalm 45

D
A
Y

2
8

_____

_____

_____

_____

_____

_____

_____

_____

Exodus 4–5   Leviticus 4   Psalm 46

_____
_____
_____
_____
_____
_____
_____
_____

What do you see through the lens of Scripture?

Exodus 6–7   Leviticus 5   Psalm 47

_____
_____
_____
_____
_____
_____
_____

Exodus 8   Leviticus 6   Psalm 48

_____

_____

_____

_____

_____

_____

_____

What do you see through the lens of Scripture?

Exodus 9   Leviticus 7   Psalm 49

_____

_____

_____

_____

_____

_____

_____

DAY 33

Exodus 10–11   Leviticus 8   Psalm 50

_____
_____
_____
_____
_____
_____
_____

What do you see through the lens of Scripture?

DAY 34

Exodus 12   Leviticus 9   *Psalm 114*

_____
_____
_____
_____
_____
_____

Exodus 13–14   Leviticus 10   Psalm 53

_____

_____

_____

_____

_____

_____

_____

What do you see through the lens of Scripture?

Exodus 15–16   Leviticus 11   Psalm 71

_____

_____

_____

_____

_____

_____

_____

DAY 37

Exodus 17–18   Leviticus 12   Psalm 73

_____
_____
_____
_____
_____
_____
_____

What do you see through the lens of Scripture?

DAY 38

Exodus 19–20   Leviticus 13   Psalm 74

_____
_____
_____
_____
_____
_____
_____

Exodus 21   Leviticus 14   Psalm 75

DAY 39

_____
_____
_____
_____
_____
_____
_____

What do you see through the lens of Scripture?

Exodus 22   Leviticus 15   Psalm 76

DAY 40

_____
_____
_____
_____
_____
_____
_____

Exodus 23   Leviticus 16   Psalm 77

_____
_____
_____
_____
_____
_____
_____

What do you see through the lens of Scripture?

Exodus 24   Leviticus 17–18   Psalm 78

_____
_____
_____
_____
_____
_____
_____

Exodus 25–26   Leviticus 19   *Psalm 119:1-56*

_____

_____

_____

_____

_____

_____

_____

What do you see through the lens of Scripture?

Exodus 27–28   Leviticus 20   *Psalm 119:57-120*

_____

_____

_____

_____

_____

_____

_____

DAY 45

Exodus 29   Leviticus 21   *Psalm 119:121-176*

_____
_____
_____
_____
_____
_____
_____

What do you see through the lens of Scripture?

DAY 46

Exodus 30–31   Leviticus 22   *Psalm 115*

_____
_____
_____
_____
_____
_____
_____

Exodus 32   Leviticus 23   Psalm 79

_____

_____

_____

_____

_____

_____

_____

What do you see through the lens of Scripture?

Exodus 33–34   Leviticus 24   Psalm 80

_____

_____

_____

_____

_____

_____

_____

DAY 49

Exodus 35–36   Leviticus 25   Psalm 81

_____
_____
_____
_____
_____
_____
_____

What do you see through the lens of Scripture?

DAY 50

Exodus 37–38   Leviticus 26   Psalm 82

_____
_____
_____
_____
_____
_____
_____

Desert Wanderings

Israel's journey to the Promised Land is a long one as they repeatedly rebel against God and Moses. For forty years, God's people wander in the desert.

_____

_____

_____

_____

_____

_____

_____

_____

_____

_____

_____

Numbers 1   Deuteronomy 1   Psalm 84

_____

_____

_____

_____

_____

_____

_____

What do you see through the lens of Scripture?

Numbers 2   Deuteronomy 2   Psalm 85

_____

_____

_____

_____

_____

_____

_____

_____

DAY 54

Numbers 3   Deuteronomy 3   Psalm 87

_____
_____
_____
_____
_____
_____
_____

What do you see through the lens of Scripture?

DAY 55

Numbers 4   Deuteronomy 4   Psalm 88

_____
_____
_____
_____
_____
_____
_____

Numbers 5   Deuteronomy 5   Psalm 90

DAY 56

_____

_____

_____

_____

_____

_____

_____

What do you see through the lens of Scripture?

Numbers 6   Deuteronomy 6   Psalm 91

DAY 57

_____

_____

_____

_____

_____

_____

DAY 58

Numbers 7   Deuteronomy 7   Psalm 92

_____
_____
_____
_____
_____
_____
_____

What do you see through the lens of Scripture?

DAY 59

Numbers 8-9   Deuteronomy 8   Psalm 93

_____
_____
_____
_____
_____
_____
_____

Numbers 10   Deuteronomy 9   Psalm 10

D
A
Y

6
0

What do you see through the lens of Scripture?

Numbers 11   Deuteronomy 10   Psalm 33

D
A
Y

6
1

Numbers 12–13   Deuteronomy 11   Psalm 94

_____
_____
_____
_____
_____
_____
_____

What do you see through the lens of Scripture?

Numbers 14   Deuteronomy 12   Psalm 95

_____
_____
_____
_____
_____
_____
_____

_____

_____

_____

_____

_____

_____

What do you see through the lens of Scripture?

_____

_____

_____

_____

_____

_____

DAY 66

Numbers 17   Deuteronomy 17–18   Psalm 98

_____
_____
_____
_____
_____
_____
_____

What do you see through the lens of Scripture?

DAY 67

Numbers 18   Deuteronomy 19–20   Psalm 99

_____
_____
_____
_____
_____
_____
_____

_____
_____
_____
_____
_____
_____
_____

What do you see through the lens of Scripture?

_____
_____
_____
_____
_____
_____
_____

Numbers 22   Deuteronomy 23   Psalm 105

_____
_____
_____
_____
_____
_____
_____
_____

What do you see through the lens of Scripture?

Numbers 23   Deuteronomy 24-25   Psalm 106

_____
_____
_____
_____
_____
_____
_____

Numbers 24–25   Deuteronomy 26   Psalm 107

_____
_____
_____
_____
_____
_____
_____

What do you see through the lens of Scripture?

Numbers 26   Deuteronomy 27   Psalm 111

_____
_____
_____
_____
_____
_____
_____

Numbers 27–28   Deuteronomy 28   Psalm 112

What do you see through the lens of Scripture?

Numbers 29–30   Deuteronomy 29   Psalm 113

Numbers 31   Deuteronomy 30   Psalm 116

D
A
Y

7
6

_____
_____
_____
_____
_____
_____
_____

What do you see through the lens of Scripture?

Numbers 32   Deuteronomy 31   Psalm 117

D
A
Y

7
7

_____
_____
_____
_____
_____
_____
_____

DAY 78

Numbers 33   Deuteronomy 32   Psalm 118

_____
_____
_____
_____
_____
_____
_____

What do you see through the lens of Scripture?

DAY 79

Numbers 34   Deuteronomy 33   Psalm 120

_____
_____
_____
_____
_____
_____
_____

What do you see through the lens of Scripture?

Conquest and Judges

1406 BC to 1050 BC

The Israelites finally enter the Promised Land under Joshua and conquer much of the territory, dividing the land among the twelve tribes of Israel. However, they still face their most important challenge of all: how to stay faithful to God.

What do you see through the lens of Scripture?

Joshua 8–9　　　　　　　　　　　　　　　　　　　　　　Psalm 126

_____
_____
_____
_____
_____
_____
_____

What do you see through the lens of Scripture?

Joshua 10–11　　　　　　　　　　　　　　　　　　　　Psalm 128

_____
_____
_____
_____
_____
_____
_____

Joshua 12–14

Psalm 129

D
A
Y

8
5

_____

_____

_____

_____

_____

_____

What do you see through the lens of Scripture?

Joshua 15–18

Psalm 130

D
A
Y

8
6

_____

_____

_____

_____

_____

_____

_____

Joshua 19–21

Psalm 131

_____

_____

_____

_____

_____

_____

_____

What do you see through the lens of Scripture?

Joshua 22–24

Psalm 132

_____

_____

_____

_____

_____

_____

_____

Judges 1–3   Ruth 1   Psalm 133

What do you see through the lens of Scripture?

Judges 4–5   Ruth 2   Psalm 134

D A Y 8 9

D A Y 9 0

Judges 6-8   Ruth 3   Psalm 135

_____

_____

_____

_____

_____

_____

_____

What do you see through the lens of Scripture?

Judges 9-11   Ruth 4   Psalm 137

_____

_____

_____

_____

_____

_____

_____

Judges 12–15   Psalm 146

DAY 93

What do you see through the lens of Scripture?

Judges 16–18   Psalm 147

DAY 94

Judges 19–21

Psalm 148

_____

_____

_____

_____

_____

_____

_____

What do you see through the lens of Scripture?

1 Samuel 1–2

Psalm 149

_____

_____

_____

_____

_____

_____

1 Samuel 3–5

What do you see through the lens of Scripture?

1 Samuel 6–8

Psalm 86

Messianic Checkpoint

The Savior promised to Adam and Eve is Jesus, the Messiah. Throughout the story of salvation history, God never abandons his people or forgets his promise. This Messianic Checkpoint is a reminder of his steadfast love.

_____

_____

_____

_____

_____

_____

_____

_____

_____

_____

_____

_____

John 1–3   Proverbs 5:1-6

_____
_____
_____
_____
_____
_____
_____

What do you see through the lens of Scripture?

John 4–6   Proverbs 5:7-14

_____
_____
_____
_____
_____
_____
_____

John 7–9   Proverbs 5:15-23

_____

_____

_____

_____

_____

_____

_____

What do you see through the lens of Scripture?

John 10–12   Proverbs 6:1-5

_____

_____

_____

_____

_____

_____

_____

John 13–15   Proverbs 6:6-11

_____

_____

_____

_____

_____

_____

_____

What do you see through the lens of Scripture?

John 16–18   Proverbs 6:12-15

_____

_____

_____

_____

_____

_____

_____

John 19–21   Proverbs 6:16-22

_____

_____

_____

_____

_____

_____

_____

What do you see through the lens of Scripture?

Royal Kingdom

1050 BC to 930 BC

Although Israel becomes a united kingdom under Saul, the first king of Israel, Saul is not totally devoted to God. A great warrior named David becomes the second king and brings the Ark of the Covenant to Jerusalem. God establishes a covenant with David—the Savior will be one of his descendants. When David dies, his son Solomon takes the throne and builds a splendid temple in Jerusalem.

DAY 106

1 Samuel 9–10

Proverbs 6:23-35

_____
_____
_____
_____
_____
_____
_____

What do you see through the lens of Scripture?

DAY 107

1 Samuel 11–12

Psalm 55

_____
_____
_____
_____
_____
_____
_____

1 Samuel 13–14

Psalm 58

What do you see through the lens of Scripture?

---

1 Samuel 15–16

Psalm 61

DAY 110

1 Samuel 17

Psalm 12

_____
_____
_____
_____
_____
_____
_____

What do you see through the lens of Scripture?

DAY 111

1 Samuel 18–19

Psalm 59

_____
_____
_____
_____
_____
_____
_____

1 Samuel 20

Psalm 142

_____

_____

_____

_____

_____

_____

What do you see through the lens of Scripture?

1 Samuel 21–22

Psalm 52

_____

_____

_____

_____

_____

_____

1 Samuel 23

Psalm 54

_____
_____
_____
_____
_____
_____
_____

What do you see through the lens of Scripture?

1 Samuel 24

Psalm 57

_____
_____
_____
_____
_____
_____
_____

1 Samuel 25

Psalm 63

_____
_____
_____
_____
_____
_____
_____
_____

What do you see through the lens of Scripture?

1 Samuel 26

Psalm 56

_____
_____
_____
_____
_____
_____
_____

DAY 118

1 Samuel 27–28

Psalm 34

_____

_____

_____

_____

_____

_____

_____

What do you see through the lens of Scripture?

DAY 119

1 Samuel 29–31

Psalm 18

_____

_____

_____

_____

_____

_____

2 Samuel 1   1 Chronicles 1   Psalm 13

_____
_____
_____
_____
_____
_____
_____

What do you see through the lens of Scripture?

2 Samuel 2   1 Chronicles 2   Psalm 24

_____
_____
_____
_____
_____
_____
_____

DAY 122

2 Samuel 3   1 Chronicles 3–4   Psalm 25

_____
_____
_____
_____
_____
_____
_____

What do you see through the lens of Scripture?

DAY 123

2 Samuel 4   1 Chronicles 5–6   Psalm 26

_____
_____
_____
_____
_____
_____

2 Samuel 5   1 Chronicles 7–8   Psalm 27

What do you see through the lens of Scripture?

2 Samuel 6-7   1 Chronicles 9   _Psalm 89_

DAY 126

2 Samuel 8   1 Chronicles 10–11   *Psalm 60*

_____
_____
_____
_____
_____
_____
_____

What do you see through the lens of Scripture?

DAY 127

2 Samuel 9   1 Chronicles 12   Psalm 28

_____
_____
_____
_____
_____
_____

2 Samuel 10   1 Chronicles 13   Psalm 31

_____

_____

_____

_____

_____

_____

_____

What do you see through the lens of Scripture?

2 Samuel 11   1 Chronicles 14–15   Psalm 32

_____

_____

_____

_____

_____

_____

_____

DAY 130

2 Samuel 12   1 Chronicles 16   *Psalm 51*

_____
_____
_____
_____
_____
_____
_____

What do you see through the lens of Scripture?

DAY 131

2 Samuel 13   1 Chronicles 17   Psalm 35

_____
_____
_____
_____
_____
_____
_____

2 Samuel 14   1 Chronicles 18   Psalm 14

What do you see through the lens of Scripture?

2 Samuel 15   1 Chronicles 19–20   _Psalm 3_

2 Samuel 16   1 Chronicles 21   Psalm 15

_____
_____
_____
_____
_____
_____
_____

What do you see through the lens of Scripture?

2 Samuel 17   1 Chronicles 22   Psalm 36

_____
_____
_____
_____
_____
_____
_____

2 Samuel 18   1 Chronicles 23   Psalm 37

What do you see through the lens of Scripture?

2 Samuel 19   1 Chronicles 24   Psalm 38

2 Samuel 20   1 Chronicles 25   Psalm 39

_____
_____
_____
_____
_____
_____
_____

What do you see through the lens of Scripture?

2 Samuel 21   1 Chronicles 26   Psalm 40

_____
_____
_____
_____
_____
_____
_____

2 Samuel 22   1 Chronicles 27   Psalm 41

_____

_____

_____

_____

_____

_____

_____

What do you see through the lens of Scripture?

2 Samuel 23   1 Chronicles 28   Psalm 42

_____

_____

_____

_____

_____

_____

_____

2 Samuel 24   1 Chronicles 29   *Psalm 30*

_____
_____
_____
_____
_____
_____
_____
_____

What do you see through the lens of Scripture?

1 Kings 1   2 Chronicles 1   Psalm 43

_____
_____
_____
_____
_____
_____
_____

1 Kings 2   2 Chronicles 2–3   Psalm 62

_____

_____

_____

_____

_____

_____

_____

What do you see through the lens of Scripture?

1 Kings 3   2 Chronicles 4–5   Psalm 64

_____

_____

_____

_____

_____

_____

1 Kings 4   2 Chronicles 6   Psalm 65

_____

_____

_____

_____

_____

_____

_____

What do you see through the lens of Scripture?

1 Kings 5   2 Chronicles 7–8   Psalm 66

_____

_____

_____

_____

_____

_____

_____

1 Kings 6   2 Chronicles 9   Psalm 4

_____
_____
_____
_____
_____
_____
_____
_____

What do you see through the lens of Scripture?

1 Kings 7   Ecclesiastes 1–2   Psalm 5

_____
_____
_____
_____
_____
_____
_____
_____

DAY 150

1 Kings 8	Ecclesiastes 3–5	Psalm 6

_____

_____

_____

_____

_____

_____

_____

What do you see through the lens of Scripture?

DAY 151

1 Kings 9	Ecclesiastes 6–7	Psalm 7

_____

_____

_____

_____

_____

_____

_____

1 Kings 10 Ecclesiastes 8–9 Psalm 8

DAY 152

What do you see through the lens of Scripture?

1 Kings 11 Ecclesiastes 10–12 Psalm 9

DAY 153

Messianic Checkpoint

_____

_____

_____

_____

_____

_____

_____

_____

_____

_____

_____

Mark 1–2   Psalm 11

_____
_____
_____
_____
_____
_____
_____
_____

What do you see through the lens of Scripture?

Mark 3–4   Psalm 20

_____
_____
_____
_____
_____
_____
_____
_____

DAY 156

Mark 5–6

Psalm 21

_____
_____
_____
_____
_____
_____
_____
_____

What do you see through the lens of Scripture?

DAY 157

Mark 7–8

Psalm 23

_____
_____
_____
_____
_____
_____
_____
_____

Mark 9–10   Psalm 29

_____

_____

_____

_____

_____

_____

_____

What do you see through the lens of Scripture?

Mark 11–12   Psalm 67

_____

_____

_____

_____

_____

_____

Mark 13–14   Psalm 68

_____
_____
_____
_____
_____
_____
_____

What do you see through the lens of Scripture?

Mark 15–16   Psalm 22

_____
_____
_____
_____
_____
_____
_____
_____

Divided Kingdom

930 BC to 722 BC

Ten tribes of Israel revolt and become the Northern Kingdom. Many kings of this period are unjust and unfaithful to God, but great prophets like Elijah continue to call the people back to God.

1 Kings 12   2 Chronicles 10–11   Song of Solomon 1

_____
_____
_____
_____
_____
_____
_____
_____

What do you see through the lens of Scripture?

1 Kings 13   2 Chronicles 12–13   Song of Solomon 2

_____
_____
_____
_____
_____
_____
_____

1 Kings 14   2 Chronicles 14–15   Song of Solomon 3

_____
_____
_____
_____
_____
_____
_____

What do you see through the lens of Scripture?

1 Kings 15–16   2 Chronicles 16–17   Song of Solomon 4

_____
_____
_____
_____
_____
_____

1 Kings 17–18 2 Chronicles 18–19 Song of Solomon 5

_____
_____
_____
_____
_____
_____
_____
_____

What do you see through the lens of Scripture?

1 Kings 19–20 2 Chronicles 20 Song of Solomon 6

_____
_____
_____
_____
_____
_____

1 Kings 21

2 Chronicles 21–22

Song of Solomon 7

What do you see through the lens of Scripture?

---

1 Kings 22

2 Chronicles 23

Song of Solomon 8

2 Kings 1   2 Chronicles 24   Psalm 69

_____

_____

_____

_____

_____

_____

_____

What do you see through the lens of Scripture?

2 Kings 2   2 Chronicles 25   Psalm 70

_____

_____

_____

_____

_____

_____

_____

_____

_____

_____

_____

_____

_____

What do you see through the lens of Scripture?

_____

_____

_____

_____

_____

_____

_____

2 Kings 5   Hosea 1–3   Psalm 101

_____

_____

_____

_____

_____

_____

_____

What do you see through the lens of Scripture?

2 Kings 6–7   Hosea 4–7   Psalm 103

_____

_____

_____

_____

_____

_____

_____

2 Kings 8   Hosea 8–10   Psalm 108

What do you see through the lens of Scripture?

---

2 Kings 9   Hosea 11–14   Psalm 109

2 Kings 10   Amos 1–3   Psalm 110

_____
_____
_____
_____
_____
_____
_____

What do you see through the lens of Scripture?

2 Kings 11–12   Amos 4–6   Psalm 122

_____
_____
_____
_____
_____
_____
_____

2 Kings 13-14   Amos 7-9   Psalm 124

_____

_____

_____

_____

_____

_____

_____

What do you see through the lens of Scripture?

2 Kings 15   Jonah 1-4   Psalm 138

_____

_____

_____

_____

_____

_____

_____

D A Y 1 8 2

2 Kings 16   Micah 1–4   Psalm 139

_____
_____
_____
_____
_____
_____
_____

What do you see through the lens of Scripture?

D A Y 1 8 3

2 Kings 17   Micah 5–7   Psalm 140

_____
_____
_____
_____
_____
_____
_____

Exile

The Northern Kingdom of Israel falls to Assyria in the year 722 BC. A century and a half later, Babylon defeats the Southern Kingdom and destroys the Temple. During the upheaval and the exile that follows, the prophets remind the Israelites that God will not abandon them.

DAY 184

2 Kings 18 2 Chronicles 29 Psalm 141

_____
_____
_____
_____
_____
_____
_____

What do you see through the lens of Scripture?

DAY 185

2 Kings 19 2 Chronicles 30 Psalm 143

_____
_____
_____
_____
_____
_____
_____

_____
_____
_____
_____
_____
_____
_____

What do you see through the lens of Scripture?

_____
_____
_____
_____
_____
_____
_____

DAY 188

2 Kings 22   2 Chronicles 33   Proverbs 7

_____
_____
_____
_____
_____
_____
_____

What do you see through the lens of Scripture?

DAY 189

2 Kings 23   2 Chronicles 34   Proverbs 8:1-21

_____
_____
_____
_____
_____
_____
_____

2 Kings 24   2 Chronicles 35   Proverbs 8:22-36

DAY 190

_____
_____
_____
_____
_____
_____
_____

What do you see through the lens of Scripture?

2 Kings 25   2 Chronicles 36   Proverbs 9:1-6

DAY 191

_____
_____
_____
_____
_____
_____
_____

DAY 192

Isaiah 1–2   Tobit 1–2   Proverbs 9:7-12

_____
_____
_____
_____
_____
_____
_____
_____

What do you see through the lens of Scripture?

DAY 193

Isaiah 3–4   Tobit 3–4   Proverbs 9:13-18

_____
_____
_____
_____
_____
_____
_____
_____

Isaiah 5–6   Tobit 5–6   Proverbs 10:1-4

_____

_____

_____

_____

_____

_____

_____

What do you see through the lens of Scripture?

Isaiah 7–8   Tobit 7–9   Proverbs 10:5-8

_____

_____

_____

_____

_____

_____

_____

DAY 1966

Isaiah 9–10   Tobit 10–12   Proverbs 10:9-12

_____
_____
_____
_____
_____
_____
_____

What do you see through the lens of Scripture?

DAY 1977

Isaiah 11–13   Tobit 13–14   Proverbs 10:13-16

_____
_____
_____
_____
_____
_____
_____

Isaiah 14–15   Joel 1–2   Proverbs 10:17-20

_____
_____
_____
_____
_____
_____
_____

What do you see through the lens of Scripture?

Isaiah 16–17   Joel 3   Proverbs 10:21-24

_____
_____
_____
_____
_____
_____
_____

DAY 200

Isaiah 18–20   Nahum 1–2   Proverbs 10:25-28

_____
_____
_____
_____
_____
_____
_____

What do you see through the lens of Scripture?

DAY 201

Isaiah 21–22   Nahum 3   Proverbs 10:29-32

_____
_____
_____
_____
_____
_____
_____

Isaiah 23–24   Habakkuk 1–2   Proverbs 11:1-4

_____
_____
_____
_____
_____
_____
_____

What do you see through the lens of Scripture?

Isaiah 25–27   Habakkuk 3   Proverbs 11:5-8

_____
_____
_____
_____
_____
_____
_____

Isaiah 28–29   Zephaniah 1–2   Proverbs 11:9-12

What do you see through the lens of Scripture?

Isaiah 30–31   Zephaniah 3   Proverbs 11:13-16

Isaiah 32–33   Baruch 1–2   Proverbs 11:17-20

_____

_____

_____

_____

_____

_____

What do you see through the lens of Scripture?

Isaiah 34–36   Baruch 3–4   Proverbs 11:21-24

_____

_____

_____

_____

_____

_____

_____

Isaiah 37–38   Baruch 5–6   Proverbs 11:25-28

_____

_____

_____

_____

_____

_____

_____

What do you see through the lens of Scripture?

Isaiah 39–40   Ezekiel 1   Proverbs 11:29-31

_____

_____

_____

_____

_____

_____

_____

_____
_____
_____
_____
_____
_____
_____

What do you see through the lens of Scripture?

_____
_____
_____
_____
_____
_____
_____

Isaiah 45–46   Ezekiel 6–7   Proverbs 12:9-12

_____
_____
_____
_____
_____
_____
_____

What do you see through the lens of Scripture?

Isaiah 47–48   Ezekiel 8–9   Proverbs 12:13-16

_____
_____
_____
_____
_____
_____
_____

Isaiah 49–50   Ezekiel 10–11   Proverbs 12:17-20

_____

_____

_____

_____

_____

_____

_____

What do you see through the lens of Scripture?

Isaiah 51–52   Ezekiel 12–13   Proverbs 12:21-24

_____

_____

_____

_____

_____

_____

_____

Isaiah 53–54   Ezekiel 14–15   Proverbs 12:25-28

_____

_____

_____

_____

_____

_____

_____

What do you see through the lens of Scripture?

Isaiah 55–56   Ezekiel 16   Proverbs 13:1-4

_____

_____

_____

_____

_____

_____

_____

Isaiah 57–58   Ezekiel 17–18   Proverbs 13:5-8

_____
_____
_____
_____
_____
_____
_____

What do you see through the lens of Scripture?

Isaiah 59–60   Ezekiel 19   Proverbs 13:9-12

DAY 219

_____
_____
_____
_____
_____
_____
_____

Isaiah 61–62   Ezekiel 20   Proverbs 13:13-16

_____
_____
_____
_____
_____
_____
_____

What do you see through the lens of Scripture?

Isaiah 63–64   Ezekiel 21–22   Proverbs 13:17-20

_____
_____
_____
_____
_____
_____
_____

Isaiah 65   Ezekiel 23–24   Proverbs 13:21-25

What do you see through the lens of Scripture?

Isaiah 66   Ezekiel 25–26   Proverbs 14:1-4

D A Y 2 2 4

Jeremiah 1   Ezekiel 27   Proverbs 14:5-8

_____
_____
_____
_____
_____
_____
_____

What do you see through the lens of Scripture?

D A Y 2 2 5

Jeremiah 2   Ezekiel 28   Proverbs 14:9-12

_____
_____
_____
_____
_____
_____
_____

Jeremiah 3　　　　　　Ezekiel 29–30　　　　　　Proverbs 14:13-16

What do you see through the lens of Scripture?

Jeremiah 4　　　　　　Ezekiel 31–32　　　　　　Proverbs 14:17-20

Jeremiah 5   Ezekiel 33   Proverbs 14:21-24

_____
_____
_____
_____
_____
_____
_____
_____

What do you see through the lens of Scripture?

Jeremiah 6   Ezekiel 34–35   Proverbs 14:25-28

_____
_____
_____
_____
_____
_____
_____
_____

_____
_____
_____
_____
_____
_____
_____

What do you see through the lens of Scripture?

_____
_____
_____
_____
_____
_____
_____

Jeremiah 9   Ezekiel 39   Proverbs 15:1-4

_____

_____

_____

_____

_____

_____

_____

What do you see through the lens of Scripture?

Jeremiah 10–11   Ezekiel 40   Proverbs 15:5-8

_____

_____

_____

_____

_____

_____

_____

Jeremiah 12–13   Ezekiel 41–42   Proverbs 15:9-12

_____

_____

_____

_____

_____

_____

_____

What do you see through the lens of Scripture?

Jeremiah 14–15   Ezekiel 43–44   Proverbs 15:13-16

_____

_____

_____

_____

_____

_____

DAY 236

Jeremiah 16–17   Ezekiel 45–46   Proverbs 15:17-20

_____
_____
_____
_____
_____
_____
_____
_____

What do you see through the lens of Scripture?

DAY 237

Jeremiah 18–19   Ezekiel 47–48   Proverbs 15:21-24

_____
_____
_____
_____
_____
_____
_____
_____

What do you see through the lens of Scripture?

_____

_____

_____

_____

_____

_____

_____

_____

What do you see through the lens of Scripture?

_____

_____

_____

_____

_____

_____

_____

_____

_____
_____
_____
_____
_____
_____
_____

What do you see through the lens of Scripture?

_____
_____
_____
_____
_____
_____
_____

DAY 244

Jeremiah 30   Daniel 12–13   Proverbs 16:17-20

_____

_____

_____

_____

_____

_____

_____

What do you see through the lens of Scripture?

DAY 245

Jeremiah 31   Daniel 14   Proverbs 16:21-24

_____

_____

_____

_____

_____

_____

_____

Jeremiah 32   Judith 1–2   Proverbs 16:25-28

_____
_____
_____
_____
_____
_____
_____

What do you see through the lens of Scripture?

Jeremiah 33–34   Judith 3–5   Proverbs 16:29-33

_____
_____
_____
_____
_____
_____
_____

Jeremiah 35–36 Judith 6–7 Proverbs 17:1-4

_____

_____

_____

_____

_____

_____

_____

What do you see through the lens of Scripture?

Jeremiah 37–38 Judith 8–9 Proverbs 17:5-8

_____

_____

_____

_____

_____

_____

_____

Jeremiah 39–40   Judith 10–11   Proverbs 17:9-12

_____

_____

_____

_____

_____

_____

_____

What do you see through the lens of Scripture?

Jeremiah 41–42   Judith 12–14   Proverbs 17:13-16

_____

_____

_____

_____

_____

_____

_____

Jeremiah 43–44   Judith 15–16   Proverbs 17:17-20

_____

_____

_____

_____

_____

_____

_____

What do you see through the lens of Scripture?

Jeremiah 45–46   Lamentations 1   Proverbs 17:21-28

_____

_____

_____

_____

_____

_____

_____

Jeremiah 47–48   Lamentations 2   Proverbs 18:1-4

What do you see through the lens of Scripture?

Jeremiah 49–50   Lamentations 3   Proverbs 18:5-8

DAY 256

Jeremiah 51   Lamentations 4–5   Proverbs 18:9-12

_____
_____
_____
_____
_____
_____
_____

What do you see through the lens of Scripture?

DAY 257

Jeremiah 52   Obadiah   Proverbs 18:13-16

_____
_____
_____
_____
_____
_____

Messianic Checkpoint

Matthew 1–4

Proverbs 18:17-20

_____
_____
_____
_____
_____
_____
_____
_____

What do you see through the lens of Scripture?

Matthew 5–7

Proverbs 18:21-24

_____
_____
_____
_____
_____
_____
_____
_____

Matthew 8–10   Proverbs 19:1-4

_____
_____
_____
_____
_____
_____
_____

What do you see through the lens of Scripture?

Matthew 11–13   Proverbs 19:5-8

_____
_____
_____
_____
_____
_____
_____

DAY 262

Matthew 14–17

Proverbs 19:9-12

What do you see through the lens of Scripture?

DAY 263

Matthew 18–21

Proverbs 19:13-16

Matthew 22–24   Proverbs 19:17-20

DAY

2
6
4

_____

_____

_____

_____

_____

_____

What do you see through the lens of Scripture?

Matthew 25–26   Proverbs 19:21-24

DAY

2
6
5

_____

_____

_____

_____

_____

_____

Matthew 27–28

Proverbs 19:25-29

What do you see through the lens of Scripture?

Return

After decades of exile, the Israelites are allowed to return to their homeland, where they rebuild the Temple in Jerusalem. Although it is difficult, key leaders and prophets guide the people to rebuild the city and their lives according to God's Law.

_____

_____

_____

_____

_____

_____

_____

_____

_____

_____

_____

DAY 267

Ezra 1–2   Haggai 1–2   Proverbs 20:1-3

What do you see through the lens of Scripture?

DAY 268

Ezra 3–4   Zechariah 1–3   Proverbs 20:4-7

_____

_____

_____

_____

_____

_____

_____

What do you see through the lens of Scripture?

_____

_____

_____

_____

_____

_____

_____

DAY 271

Ezra 9–10   Zechariah 9–11   Proverbs 20:16-19

_____

_____

_____

_____

_____

_____

_____

What do you see through the lens of Scripture?

DAY 272

Nehemiah 1–2   Zechariah 12–13   Proverbs 20:20-22

_____

_____

_____

_____

_____

_____

_____

Nehemiah 3   Zechariah 14   Proverbs 20:23-26

What do you see through the lens of Scripture?

Nehemiah 4-5   Esther 11-12   Proverbs 20:27-30

Nehemiah 6–7   Esther 1–2   Proverbs 21:1-4

_____
_____
_____
_____
_____
_____
_____

What do you see through the lens of Scripture?

Nehemiah 8   Esther 3, 13   Proverbs 21:5-8

_____
_____
_____
_____
_____
_____
_____

What do you see through the lens of Scripture?

DAY 279

Nehemiah 11   Esther 8, 16   Proverbs 21:17-20

_____

_____

_____

_____

_____

_____

_____

What do you see through the lens of Scripture?

DAY 280

Nehemiah 12   Esther 9–11   Proverbs 21:21-24

_____

_____

_____

_____

_____

_____

_____

What do you see through the lens of Scripture?

Maccabean Revolt

The Greek ruler Antiochus tries to destroy the Israelites, but a small army of Israelites known as the Maccabees revolts and drives the Greeks out of Jerusalem. Israel becomes an independent kingdom again for about a hundred years, until the Romans take over in 63 BC.

1 Maccabees 1   Sirach 1–3   Proverbs 21:29-31

What do you see through the lens of Scripture?

1 Maccabees 2   Sirach 4–6   Proverbs 22:1-4

1 Maccabees 3   Sirach 7–9   Proverbs 22:5-8

_____
_____
_____
_____
_____
_____
_____
_____

What do you see through the lens of Scripture?

1 Maccabees 4   Sirach 10–12   Proverbs 22:9-12

_____
_____
_____
_____
_____
_____
_____
_____

1 Maccabees 5   Sirach 13–15   Proverbs 22:13-16

What do you see through the lens of Scripture?

1 Maccabees 6   Sirach 16–18   Proverbs 22:17-21

DAY 288

1 Maccabees 7 Sirach 19–21 Proverbs 22:22-25

What do you see through the lens of Scripture?

DAY 289

1 Maccabees 8 Sirach 22–23 Proverbs 22:26-29

1 Maccabees 9   Sirach 24–25   Proverbs 23:1-4

_____
_____
_____
_____
_____
_____
_____

What do you see through the lens of Scripture?

1 Maccabees 10   Sirach 26–27   Proverbs 23:5-8

_____
_____
_____
_____
_____
_____
_____

1 Maccabees 11   Sirach 28–29   Proverbs 23:9-12

_____

_____

_____

_____

_____

_____

_____

What do you see through the lens of Scripture?

1 Maccabees 12   Sirach 30–31   Proverbs 23:13-16

_____

_____

_____

_____

_____

_____

_____

1 Maccabees 13

Sirach 32–33

Proverbs 23:17-21

_____
_____
_____
_____
_____
_____
_____

What do you see through the lens of Scripture?

1 Maccabees 14

Sirach 34–35

Proverbs 23:22-25

DAY 295

_____
_____
_____
_____
_____
_____

1 Maccabees 15   Sirach 36–37   Proverbs 23:26-28

_____

_____

_____

_____

_____

_____

_____

What do you see through the lens of Scripture?

1 Maccabees 16   Sirach 38–39   Proverbs 23:29-35

_____

_____

_____

_____

_____

_____

_____

2 Maccabees 1   Sirach 40–41   Proverbs 24:1-7

What do you see through the lens of Scripture?

2 Maccabees 2   Sirach 42–44   Proverbs 24:8-9

2 Maccabees 3   Sirach 45–46   Proverbs 24:10-12

_____

_____

_____

_____

_____

_____

_____

What do you see through the lens of Scripture?

2 Maccabees 4   Sirach 47–49   Proverbs 24:13-16

_____

_____

_____

_____

_____

_____

_____

2 Maccabees 5   Sirach 50–51   Proverbs 24:17-20

What do you see through the lens of Scripture?

2 Maccabees 6   Wisdom 1–2   Proverbs 24:21-26

DAY 304

2 Maccabees 7   Wisdom 3–4   Proverbs 24:27-29

DAY 305

2 Maccabees 8   Wisdom 5–6   Proverbs 24:30-34

What do you see through the lens of Scripture?

2 Maccabees 11   Wisdom 11–12   Proverbs 25:8-10

_____

_____

_____

_____

_____

_____

_____

What do you see through the lens of Scripture?

2 Maccabees 12   Wisdom 13–14   Proverbs 25:11-14

_____

_____

_____

_____

_____

_____

_____

2 Maccabees 13   Wisdom 15–16   Proverbs 25:15-17

_____

_____

_____

_____

_____

_____

What do you see through the lens of Scripture?

2 Maccabees 14   Wisdom 17–18   Proverbs 25:18-20

_____

_____

_____

_____

_____

_____

DAY 312

2 Maccabees 15   Wisdom 19   Proverbs 25:21-23

_____

_____

_____

_____

_____

_____

_____

What do you see through the lens of Scripture?

Messianic Fulfillment

Jesus, the Son of God, becomes man in fulfillment of God's promise to Adam and Eve. Jesus calls twelve apostles and gathers many disciples as he proclaims the Good News of the kingdom, teaches, and heals many. Jesus dies on the Cross to save mankind, rises from the dead, and ascends into heaven. He establishes the New Covenant.

_____

_____

_____

_____

_____

_____

_____

_____

_____

_____

_____

DAY 313

Luke 1–2

Proverbs 25:24-26

What do you see through the lens of Scripture?

DAY 314

Luke 3–5

Proverbs 25:27-28

Luke 6–8   Proverbs 26:1-3

D
A
Y

3
1
5

What do you see through the lens of Scripture?

Luke 9–10   Proverbs 26:4-6

D
A
Y

3
1
6

Luke 11–12

Proverbs 26:7-9

What do you see through the lens of Scripture?

Luke 13–16

Proverbs 26:10-12

Luke 17–19

Proverbs 26:13-16

What do you see through the lens of Scripture?

Luke 20–22:38

Proverbs 26:17-19

DAY 321

What do you see through the lens of Scripture?

The Church

The Holy Spirit descends on the followers of Jesus, filling them with wisdom and strength. The apostles and disciples boldly proclaim the gospel to all who will listen, and Christianity spreads to the Gentiles and to many nations. Under the leadership of Peter, the Church begins its mission, which continues to this day.

DAY 322

Acts 1   Romans 1   Proverbs 26:24-26

_____
_____
_____
_____
_____
_____
_____

What do you see through the lens of Scripture?

DAY 323

Acts 2   Romans 2-3   Proverbs 26:27-28

_____
_____
_____
_____
_____
_____
_____

Acts 3   Romans 4–5   Proverbs 27:1-3

_____

_____

_____

_____

_____

_____

_____

What do you see through the lens of Scripture?

Acts 4   Romans 6–7   Proverbs 27:4-6

_____

_____

_____

_____

_____

_____

_____

DAY 326

Acts 5   Romans 8   Proverbs 27:7-9

_____
_____
_____
_____
_____
_____
_____

What do you see through the lens of Scripture?

DAY 327

Acts 6   Romans 9–10   Proverbs 27:10-12

_____
_____
_____
_____
_____
_____
_____

Acts 7   Romans 11–12   Proverbs 27:13-14

DAY 328

What do you see through the lens of Scripture?

Acts 8   Romans 13–14   Proverbs 27:15-17

DAY 329

D A Y 3 3 0

Acts 9   Romans 15–16   Proverbs 27:18-20

_____

_____

_____

_____

_____

_____

_____

What do you see through the lens of Scripture?

D A Y 3 3 1

Acts 10   1 Corinthians 1–2   Proverbs 27:21-22

_____

_____

_____

_____

_____

_____

_____

_____
_____
_____
_____
_____
_____
_____

What do you see through the lens of Scripture?

_____
_____
_____
_____
_____
_____
_____

D A Y 3 3 4

Acts 13

1 Corinthians 7–8

Proverbs 28:4-6

What do you see through the lens of Scripture?

D A Y 3 3 5

Acts 14

1 Corinthians 9–10

Proverbs 28:7-9

Acts 15   1 Corinthians 11–12   Proverbs 28:10-12

_____
_____
_____
_____
_____
_____
_____

What do you see through the lens of Scripture?

Acts 16   1 Corinthians 13–14   Proverbs 28:13-15

_____
_____
_____
_____
_____
_____
_____

**D
A
Y

3
3
8**

Acts 17   1 Corinthians 15   Proverbs 28:16-18

_____

_____

_____

_____

_____

_____

_____

What do you see through the lens of Scripture?

**D
A
Y

3
3
9**

Acts 18   1 Corinthians 16   Proverbs 28:19-21

_____

_____

_____

_____

_____

_____

_____

_____

_____

_____

_____

_____

_____

_____

What do you see through the lens of Scripture?

_____

_____

_____

_____

_____

_____

_____

DAY 342

Acts 21   2 Corinthians 6–8   Proverbs 29:1-4

_____
_____
_____
_____
_____
_____
_____

What do you see through the lens of Scripture?

DAY 343

Acts 22   2 Corinthians 9–11   Proverbs 29:5-7

_____
_____
_____
_____
_____
_____
_____

_____

_____

_____

_____

_____

_____

_____

What do you see through the lens of Scripture?

_____

_____

_____

_____

_____

_____

_____

DAY 346

Acts 25   Galatians 4–6   Proverbs 29:15-17

_____
_____
_____
_____
_____
_____
_____

What do you see through the lens of Scripture?

DAY 347

Acts 26   Ephesians 1–3   Proverbs 29:18-21

_____
_____
_____
_____
_____
_____
_____

Acts 27   Ephesians 4–6   Proverbs 29:22-24

_____
_____
_____
_____
_____
_____
_____

What do you see through the lens of Scripture?

Acts 28   Philippians 1–2   Proverbs 29:25-27

_____
_____
_____
_____
_____
_____
_____

DAY 350

James 1–2   Philippians 3–4   Proverbs 30:1–6

_____
_____
_____
_____
_____
_____
_____

What do you see through the lens of Scripture?

DAY 351

James 3–5   Colossians 1–2   Proverbs 30:7–9

_____
_____
_____
_____
_____
_____
_____

1 Peter 1–2   Colossians 3–4   Proverbs 30:10-14

DAY

3
5
2

What do you see through the lens of Scripture?

1 Peter 3–5   1 Thessalonians 1–3   Proverbs 30:15-16

DAY

3
5
3

DAY 354

2 Peter 1–3   1 Thessalonians 4–5   Proverbs 30:17-19

_____
_____
_____
_____
_____
_____
_____

What do you see through the lens of Scripture?

DAY 355

1 John 1–3   2 Thessalonians 1–3   Proverbs 30:20-23

_____
_____
_____
_____
_____
_____
_____

1 John 4–5   1 Timothy 1–3   Proverbs 30:24-28

_____
_____
_____
_____
_____
_____
_____

What do you see through the lens of Scripture?

2 John, 3 John   1 Timothy 4–6   Proverbs 30:29-33

_____
_____
_____
_____
_____
_____
_____

D A Y 3 5 8

Jude   2 Timothy 1–2   Proverbs 31:1-7

_____
_____
_____
_____
_____
_____
_____

What do you see through the lens of Scripture?

D A Y 3 5 9

Revelation 1–3   2 Timothy 3–4   Proverbs 31:8-9

_____
_____
_____
_____
_____
_____
_____

Revelation 4–7   Titus 1–3   Proverbs 31:10-15

_____
_____
_____
_____
_____
_____
_____

What do you see through the lens of Scripture?

Revelation 8–11   Philemon   Proverbs 31:16-18

_____
_____
_____
_____
_____
_____
_____

DAY 362

Revelation 12–14   Hebrews 1–4   Proverbs 31:19-22

_____
_____
_____
_____
_____
_____
_____

What do you see through the lens of Scripture?

DAY 363

Revelation 15–17   Hebrews 5–8   Proverbs 31:23-25

_____
_____
_____
_____
_____
_____
_____

Revelation 18–20   Hebrews 9–10   Proverbs 31:26-29

_____
_____
_____
_____
_____
_____
_____

What do you see through the lens of Scripture?

Revelation 21–22   Hebrews 11–13   Proverbs 31:30-31

_____
_____
_____
_____
_____
_____
_____

Congratulations!
You have completed *The Bible in a Year*!

What's **Next?**

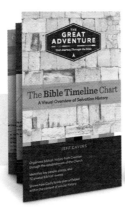
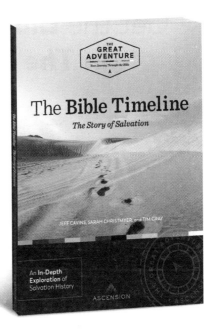